This Is My World

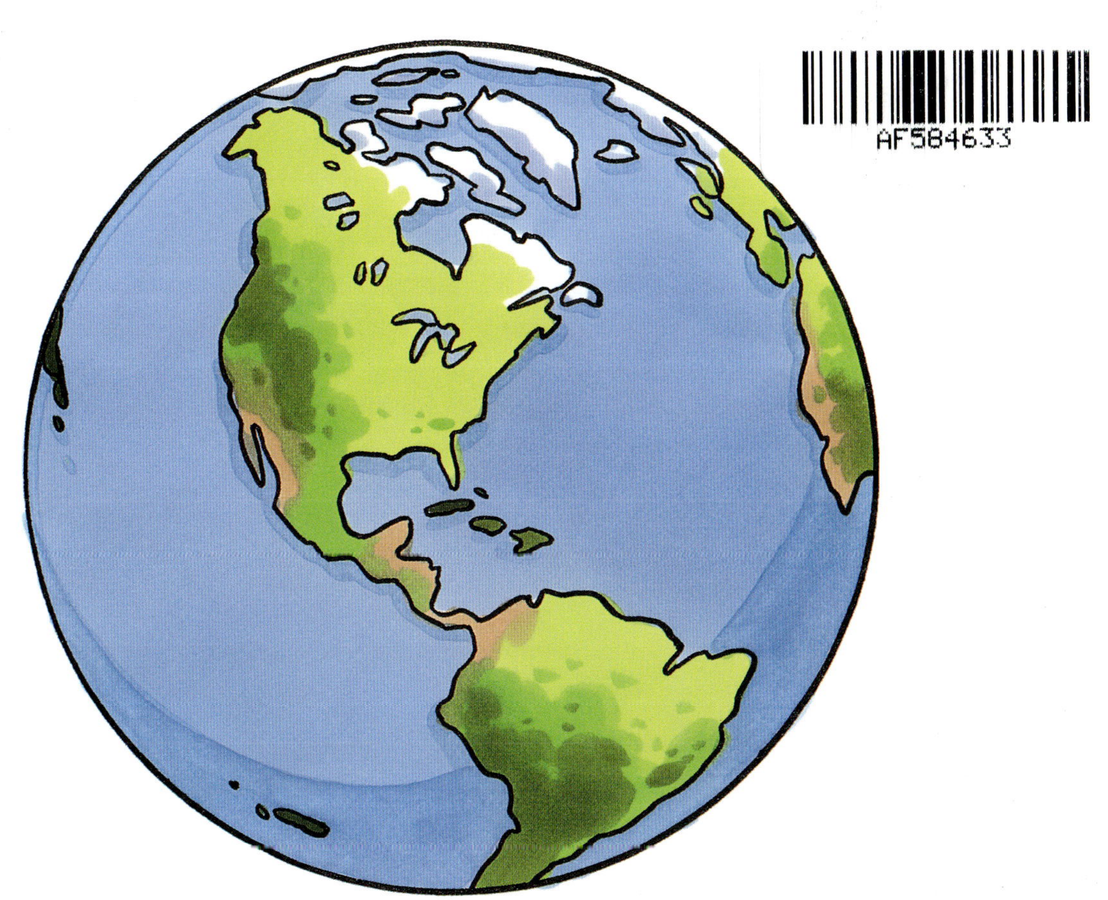

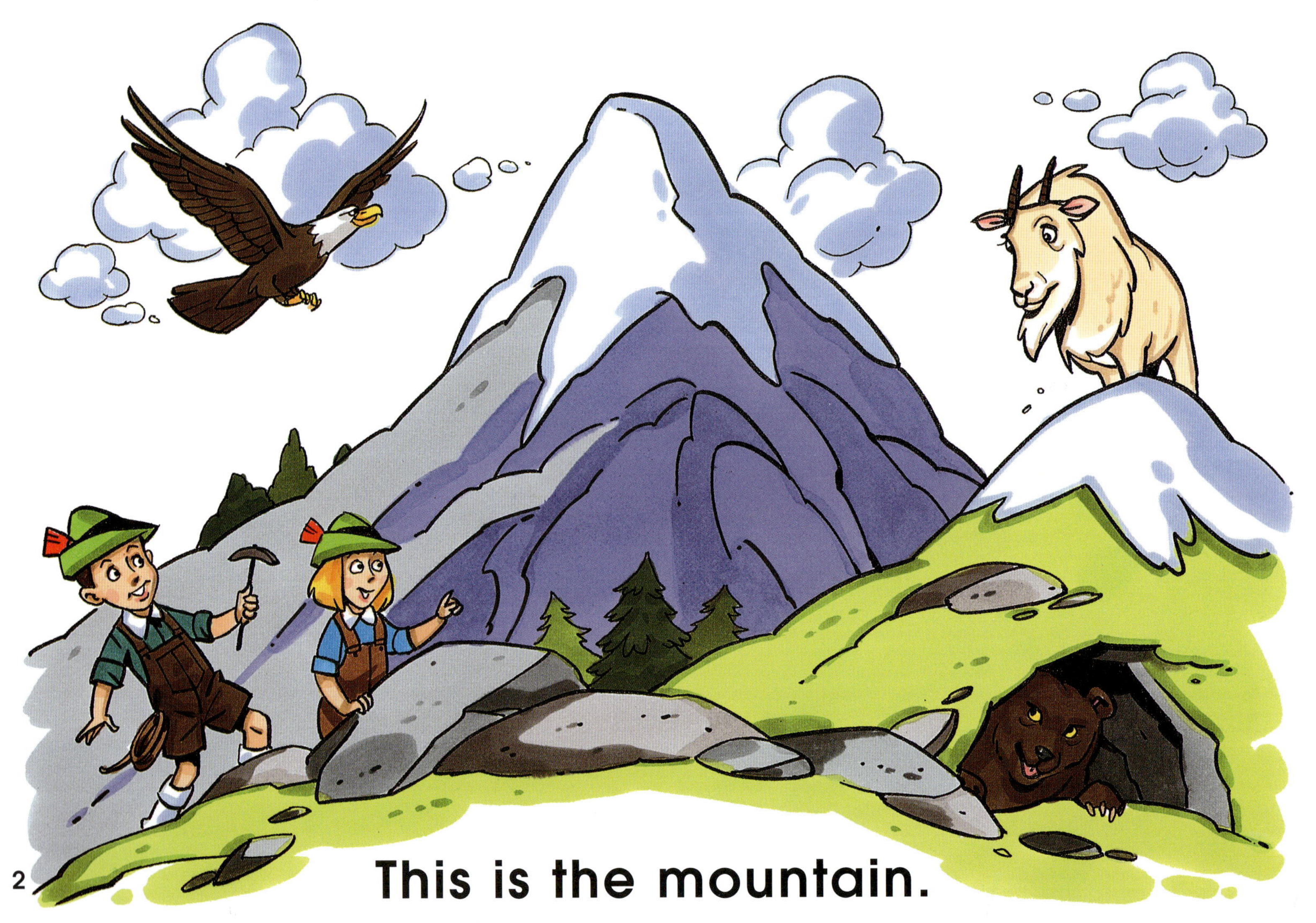

This is the mountain.

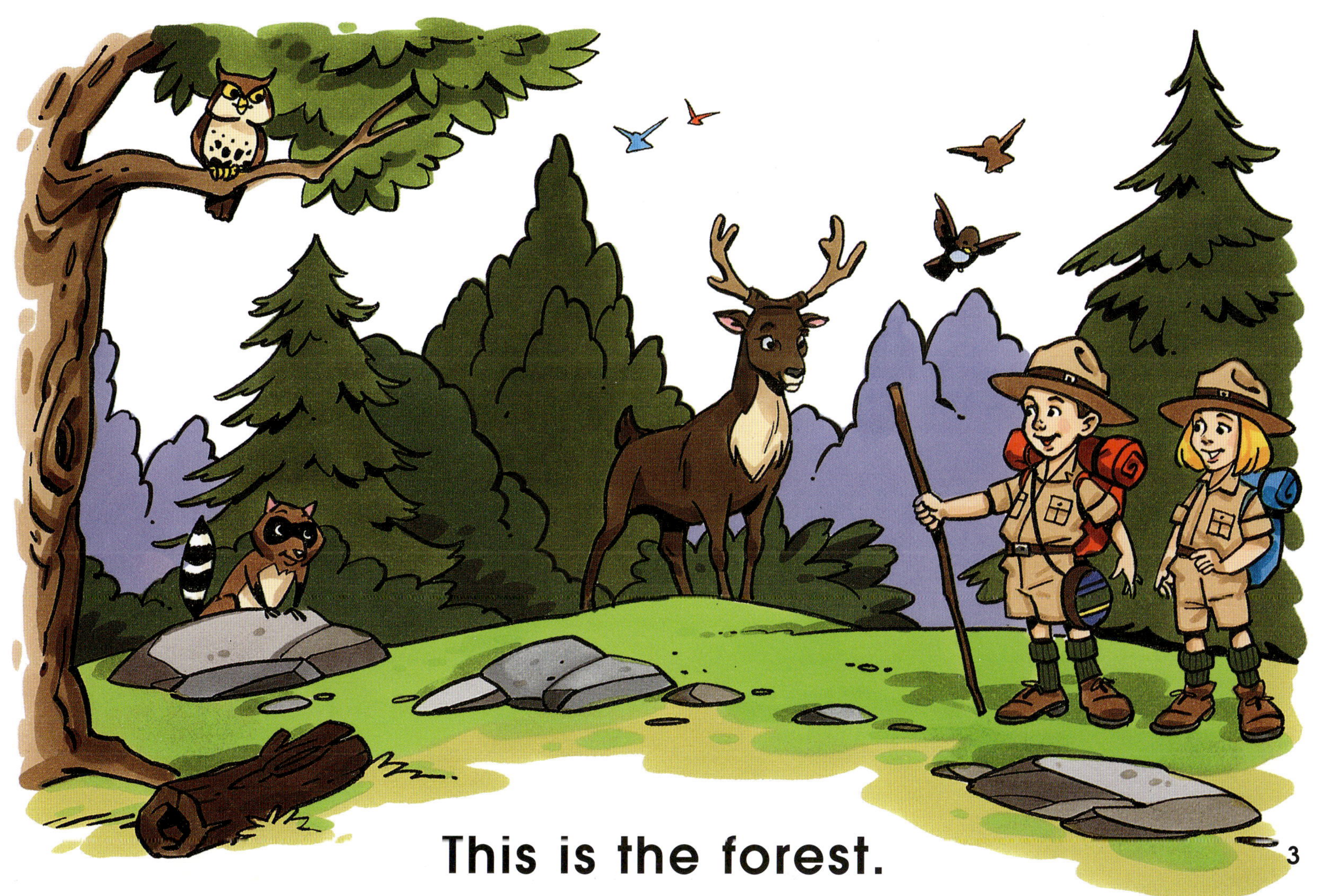

This is the forest.

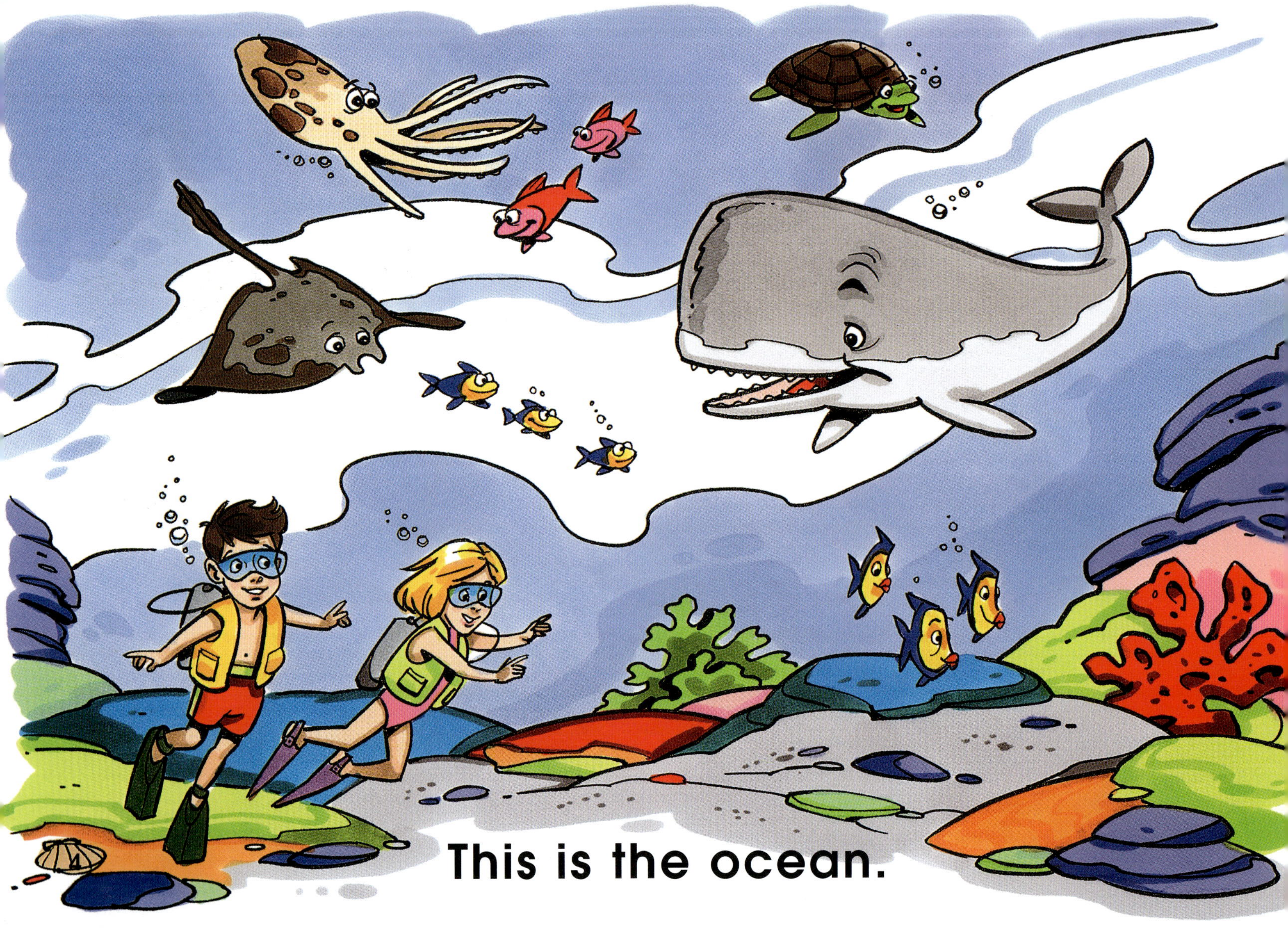

This is the ocean.

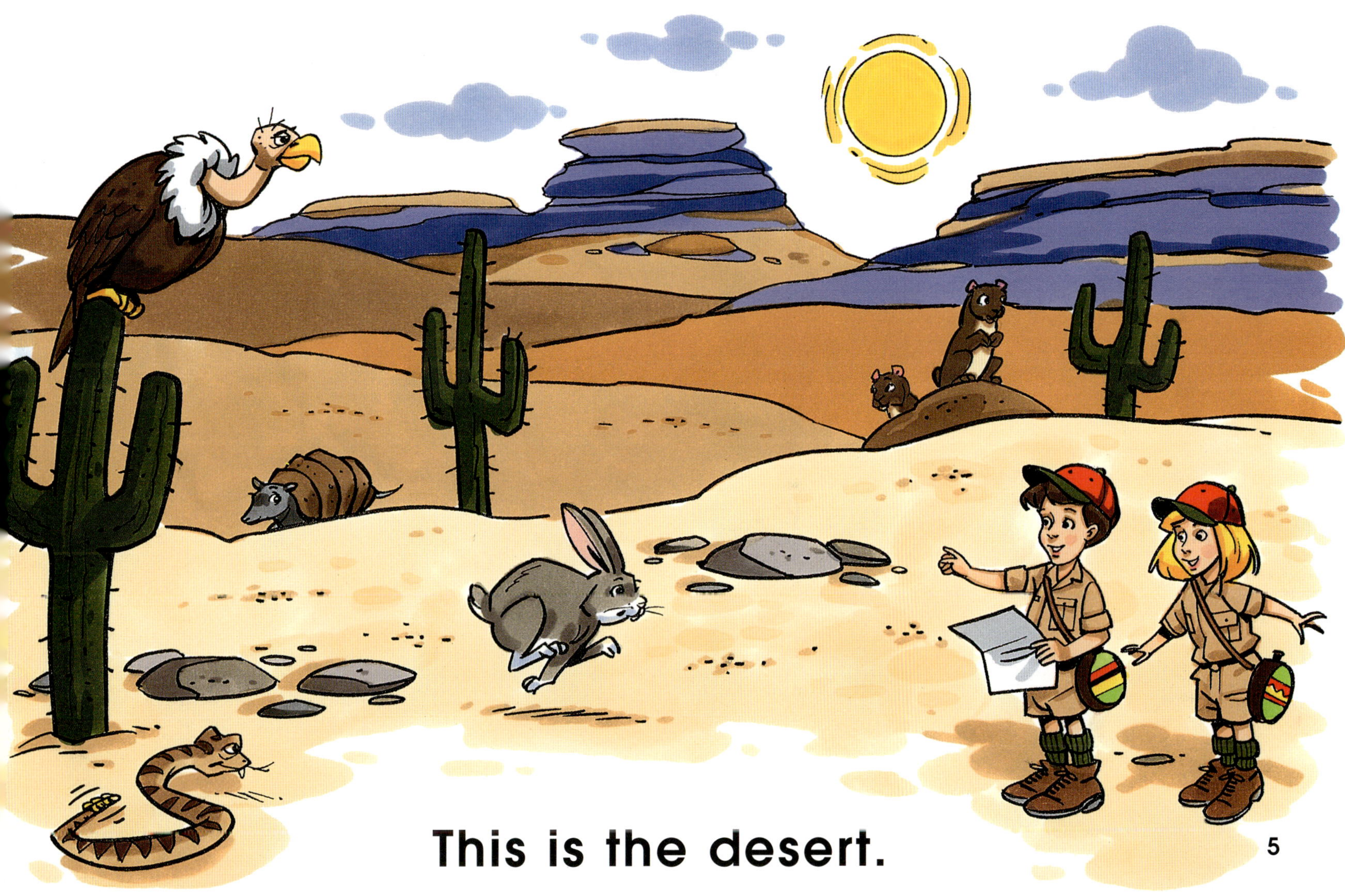

This is the desert.

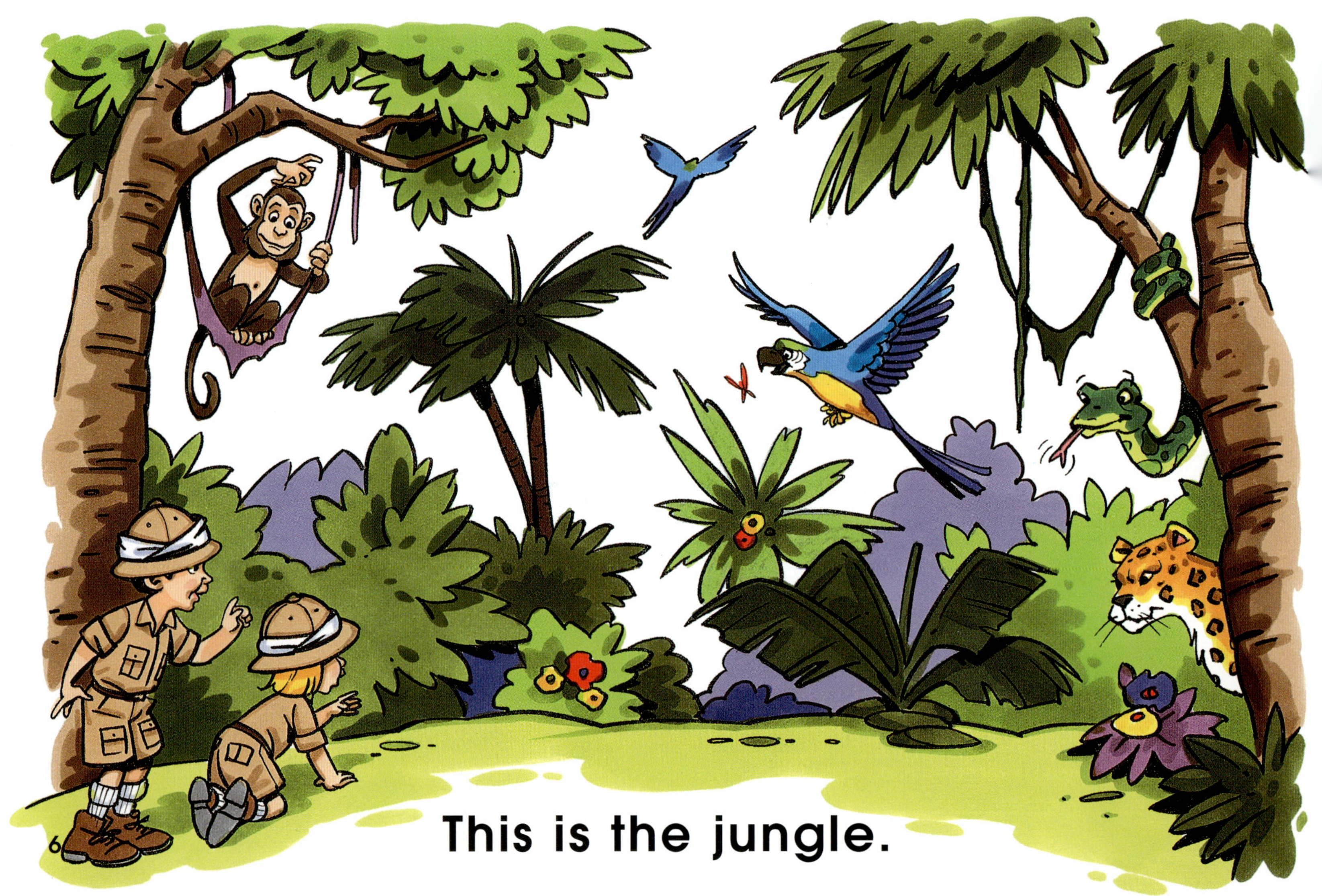

This is the jungle.

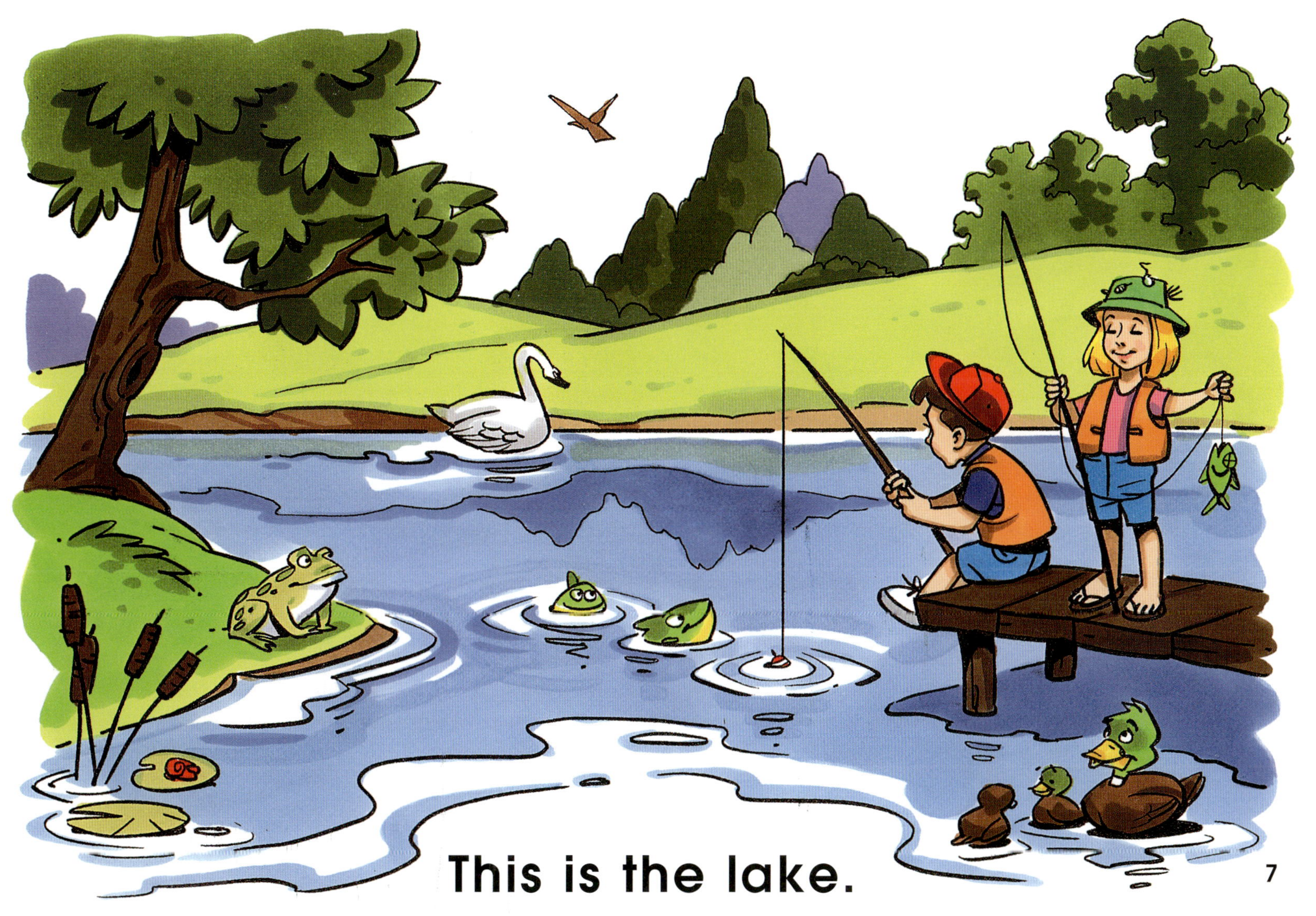

This is the lake.

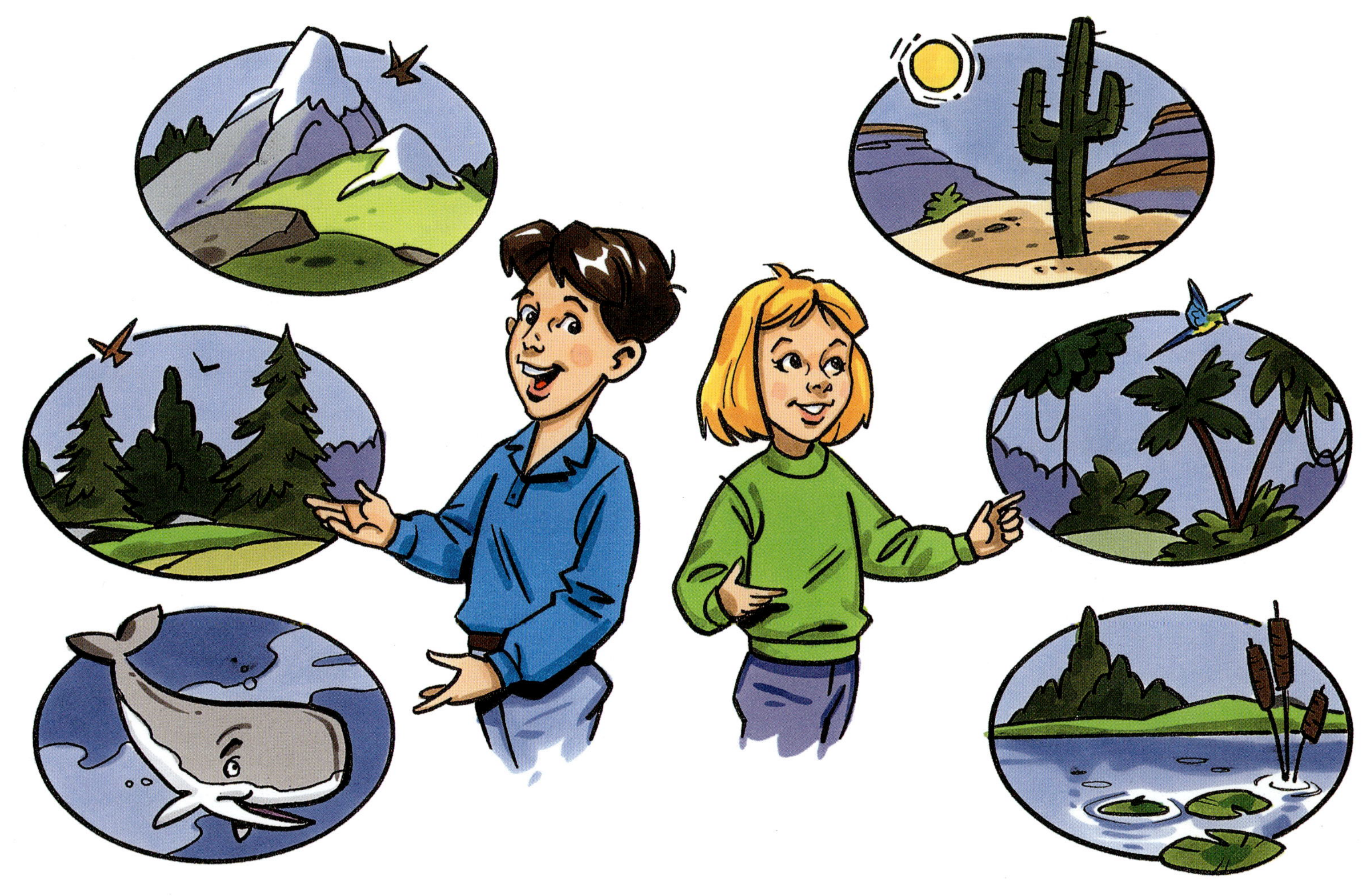

This is my world!